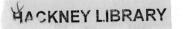

EASY PEASY LEMON SQUEEZY

COOL WAYS TO
REMEMBER STUFF

Written by Steve Martin

**Illustrated by Martin Remphry
and Michael Garton**

Edited by Jen Wainwright
Designed by Barbara Ward

EASY PEASY
LEMON SQUEEZY

COOL WAYS TO
REMEMBER STUFF

Buster Books

First published in Great Britain in 2012 by Buster Books,
an imprint of Michael O'Mara Books Limited,
9 Lion Yard, Tremadoc Road, London SW4 7NQ

www.busterbooks.co.uk

A CIP catalogue record for this book is available from the British Library.

ISBN: 978-1-78055-105-0

1 3 5 7 9 10 8 6 4 2

Printed and bound in August 2012 by Clays Limited, St Ives plc,
Popson Street, Bungay, Suffolk, NR35 1ED, UK.

Papers used by Michael O'Mara Books are natural, recyclable products
made from wood grown in sustainable forests. The manufacturing processes
conform to the environmental regulations of the country of origin.

CONTENTS

ALL ABOUT THIS BOOK

Do you sometimes sit in class wondering how the teachers expect you to remember all the information they're telling you? After all, there is just so much of it. You have to know equations for maths, stuff about yourself and other animals for science, and your geography teacher expects you to know all about everywhere!

Even when you are trying to relax at home, you're still being bombarded with information. Sports commentators will talk about the decathlon, expecting you to know which ten sports it includes. You may need to remember what currency you will need for your foreign holiday, or what you need to buy at the local shop. Arrgh!

Well, the challenge of remembering all this information and much, much more is about to get easier, as you discover a whole range of tricks to help you remember anything at all.

This book will boost your brain power by showing you how to use 'mnemonics' (pronounced ne – mon – ics), which is the fancy word for memory tricks. Here are some of the types of mnemonic you'll come across.

Rhymes

Inventing rhymes is a wonderful way of making learning and remembering both easy and fun. You can use them for anything – from learning the stages of the water cycle to the different army ranks, or from recalling the body's internal organs to how photosynthesis in plants works.

Acrostics

Acrostics are sentences that use the first letter of each word to help you remember information. You might already know some of these, such as '**R**ichard **O**f **Y**ork **G**ave **B**attle **I**n **V**ain', which is used for the colours of the rainbow (**R**ed, **O**range, **Y**ellow, **G**reen, **B**lue, **I**ndigo, **V**iolet). Later in this book, you will come across more of these. For example, you'll find out why '**A R**obber **I**n **T**he **H**ouse **M**ight **E**at **T**he **I**ce **C**ream'.

Stories

Lists of information can be much easier to remember if they are made into stories. Did you know that 'George's Car Trip' can help you learn the capital cities of South America? All will become clear when you look at the section called 'A Capital Memory' on page 62.

Grouping

Grouping facts together tricks your brain into thinking it is only learning one fact when it is really learning more. Use this book to find out about the three '**t**'s and how grouping will help you remember those ten decathlon sports!

Linking

Many mnemonics link items together to help you to remember them. For example, you won't forget that an **oct**agon has eight sides if you link it to an **oct**opus, with its eight tentacles.

Pictures

You can either draw pictures or visualize them in your imagination to fix facts in your brain. You're unlikely to forget that the Spanish word for uncle is *tio,* if you picture your uncle jumping out of his chair, yelling, 'Oh!' after spilling a cup of tea on himself.

Acronyms

An acronym is a type of mnemonic that uses the letters of what you need to remember to make up words. For example, if you look at the Super Science section (pages 80 – 91), you will see how **COG** helps you to remember the three fossil fuels (**C**oal, **O**il, **G**as), or you can visit the Language Learner section (pages 10 – 35) to find out why **BAT SWAB** is such a useful acronym.

Word Play

There are all sorts of plays on words you can use to remember things. You'll never struggle to spell 'island' again once you know that an island **is land**.

The Memory Gym

This book will make it easy for you to remember hundreds of important facts. But there's no need to stop there. You can use the techniques to create your own mnemonics to remember absolutely anything you like. The Memory Gym section at the back of the book (pages 118 – 127) will help you to practise these techniques and build up your memory muscles.

Get ready to make your memory mighty!

LANGUAGE LEARNER

HOW TO BE A SPELLING WIZARD

Even though you try your best, there are probably certain words that trip you up when you try to write them down, and cause mistakes over and over again.

Don't panic! Use the memory tricks shown here, and your spelling will improve quicker than you can say – or spell – 'Abracadabra!'

Acceptable

'Acceptable' can cause problems because you can't tell by the sound if it should end in –**able** or –**ible**. Remember the correct spelling by using the sentence:

> I am **able** to **accept** that I can spell **acceptable**.

Arithmetic

With acrostics, the sillier the sentence, the more easily it will stick in your mind. Here's one to help you remember how to spell 'arithmetic'. Remember:

> **A R**obber **I**n **T**he **H**ouse **M**ight **E**at **T**he **I**ce **C**ream.

Believe

> I do not bel**ie**ve your **lie**s.

Broccoli

My **BRO**ther **C**an't **C**hew **O**r **L**ick **I**t!

Calendar

People often forget that this word ends in –**ar**, not –**er**.
Time for some visualization …

> 👁 *Imagine you are staring at a calendar, realizing
> that you have forgotten it is your mother's birthday, and
> screaming, 'Aaaaar!'*

Now you'll never forget how to spell 'calendar' … and
hopefully you won't forget your mum's birthday, either!

Character

CHARlotte's **ACT**ing is t**ER**rible.

Forty

This play on words will help you to remember that the word 'forty' drops the letter 'u':

U may be four or fourteen, but not forty.

Friend

I'll see my **friend** on **Fri**day, at the **end** of the week.

Gauge

People struggle to remember the order of the vowels in this little word.

*Imagine walking into the cockpit of a plane and seeing someone messing with the instruments. You shout, 'A U! (Hey you!) Leave that g**au**ge alone!'*

I Before E

I before **E**, except after **C**,
Or when sounded like **A**,
As in n**ei**ghbour and w**ei**gh.

So, you'll need '**ie**' in words such as ach**ie**ve but '**ei**' in words such as de**cei**ve, **cei**ling or sl**ei**gh.

Just to be tricky, there are some exceptions to this rule. These include words such as 'spe**cies**'. There's a '**c**' in 'species', but it is still spelt with an '**ie**', because the '**c**' makes a '**sh**' sound. You will come across some other exceptions later.

Immediately

If you see a celebrity, call the **media** im**media**tely!

Island

This is easy to spell if you remember that an island **is land**.

Lose / Loose

The problem with the word 'lose' is that it is easy to confuse with 'loose', which means untied. So, remember:

One of the 'o's in l**oo**se is l**oo**se, so you might l**o**se it.

Mississippi

Mrs **M** Mrs **I** Mrs **S S I** Mrs **S S I** Mrs **P P I**

Miniature

'Miniature' means really small. Spot the two really small words in the middle of it – '**I**' and '**a**':

Min**ia**ture

Occur

The idea of crossing two seas ('**c**'s) did not o**cc**ur to me.

Ocean

Old Camels Eat Amazing Noodles.

Orangutan

To learn how to spell the word 'orangutan' without any monkeying around, remember:

Be careful you don't turn **orang**e when **u tan**!

Pastime

Some words cause spelling problems because it's difficult to know if they have double letters or not. To remember that there are no double letters in this word, use the sentence:

Pa's time is spent on his **pastime**.

Questionnaire

His **question**s were **never aire**d.

Rehearsal

At the re**hearsal**, you'll **hear Sal**ly sing.

School

Students **C**an **H**ave **O**nly **O**ne **L**emon.

Subtle

If you want to **b** su**b**tle, you have to **b** silent!

Tomorrow

We might see **Tom or Row**ena **tomorrow.**

Tongue

Tiny **O**wls **N**est **G**rumpily
Under **E**lephants.

Weird

'Weird' does not follow the famous rule – '**i**' before '**e**', except after '**c**' – so remember the spelling by the sentence:

We are so **we**ird!

Alternatively, just remember that the spelling of weird is weird because it doesn't obey the rule!

Withhold

It is really unusual to have a spelling with a double '**hh**' in the middle, which is why this spelling can look so strange. Use this sentence to help you remember it:

King **H**enry the **H**orrible wit**hh**olds his troops.

Yacht

Yellow **A**nts **C**an't **H**ave **T**oast.

SOUNDS THE SAME

Sometimes it's easy to get two or more words confused because, even though they are spelt differently, they sound the same. Words like this are called homophones. For example, if you had two pieces of a certain fruit, you might have a 'pair of pears', but you would never have a 'pear of pairs'.

Confusing? Don't worry. Here are some memory tricks that will help you avoid any mix-ups.

Alter / Altar

To 'alter' something means to change it, but an 'altar' is found in a church. Remember:

A bride shouldn't **tar**ry on her way to the al**tar**.

Beach / Beech

To tell these words apart, just remember:

You go to the b**ea**ch to swim in the s**ea**,
but a b**ee**ch is a type of tr**ee**.

Berry / Bury

To sort out the difference between these two words, remember:

A be**rr**y is **r**ipe and **r**ed.
Sc**ur**vy pirates b**ur**y treasure!

Earn / Urn

People 'earn' money by working, while an 'urn' is another word for a vase:

He started **ear**ly to **ear**n more money, so he could afford that **u**gly **u**rn his mother wanted.

Genes / Jeans

Your 'genes' are the coding in your body. They cause you to inherit certain character traits and make you who you are. They influence things such as the colour of your eyes or hair and your height. Remember:

Generally, **gene**s make you look like your relatives.

The other spelling is used for denim trousers:

Jeans are good for **j**umping around in.

Heal / Heel

A 'heel' is part of a foot, while to 'heal' something means to make it well again. Use this sentence to remember the difference:

I went to see **a** healer about my **two** heels.

Meet / Meat

Noticing the word hidden inside 'meat' can help you make sure you don't confuse these two spellings:

I'll m**ee**t you in the restaurant, where you can **eat** some m**eat**.

Mousse / Moose

A 'mousse' is a light, foamy substance. Remember:

Chocolate mou**ss**e is **s**uper **s**weet.

However, a 'moose' is a large animal with antlers.

👁 *Imagine a m**oo**se on the l**oo**se from a z**oo**.*

Piece / Peace

A 'piece' of something is a part of it. So remember the sentence:

I'd love a **pie**ce of **pie**.

'Peace' means the opposite of war. This sentence will help you to remember the spelling of this word:

Please **E**nd **A**ll **C**onflict for **E**ver.

Place / Plaice

A 'place' is a location. Use examples of places to help you remember the spelling:

Paris, **L**ondon **A**nd **C**entral **E**ngland.

The other spelling, 'plaice', is a type of fish.

Remember that 'plaice' is spelt with an '**i**' by using the sentence:

I like pla**ice**, chips and **ice** cream.

Prey / Pray

A **pre**dator eats **pre**y.
I m**ay** pr**ay** for a fine d**ay**.

Rap / Wrap

'Rap' means to beat or knock on something. With a silent 'w' in front, it means to wrap something up. Use the following sentence to help you remember the difference:

The **rap**id **rap**ping at the door interrupted him as he **wrap**ped the **w**onderful present.

Reign / Rain

To 'reign' means to be on the throne as a king or queen. The 'rain' is the wet stuff that falls from the sky. Remember:

King Henry the **Eig**hth r**eig**ned for thirty-**eig**ht years.
But even for the King, getting wet in the r**ain** is a real p**ain**!

Stair / Stare

Even when he climbs into the **air** on the st**air**s,
you **are** not to st**are** at him.

There / Their / They're

'There' is used for describing a place, as in 'over there'. You can remember this by noticing the word 'here' hidden inside the word 'there':

Look **here** and t**here**.

'Their' means it belongs to them. An 'heir' is somebody who inherits property or money. So, remember:

She will inherit **their** money because she is the **heir**.

Notice that 'their' is another pesky word that doesn't follow the '**i**' before '**e**' rule (see page 13).

'They're' is short for 'they are'. The apostrophe is used to show that there are letters missing. In this word, the '**a**' is missing:

They're learning about apostrophes.

Too / Two / To

'Too' is used when we are talking about 'too much' or 'too many' of something. Its other meaning is when it is used to mean 'also'.

£**100** is t**oo** much money. £**200** is t**oo** much money, t**oo**.

'Two' is the number 2.

👁 *Imagine* **two** *owls sitting in a tree, hooting 'Twit-two*o'.

For other uses of the word, use 'to'.

Wail / Whale

To 'wail' means to cry or scream loudly. A 'whale' is a huge mammal that swims in the ocean. Remember:

A w**h**ale has an '**h**' because it is **h**uge,
and if you heard a whale's **wail** it would be
Watery **A**nd **I**ncredibly **L**oud!

Week / Weak

I go to the gym **two e**venings a week,
but my **a**rms are still weak.

Which / Witch

Spelt with a '**t**', a witch is someone who uses magic.

👁 *Imagine an old witch in a pointy black hat sitting by her cauldron drinking a nice cup of tea (t).*

In all other cases, use the spelling 'which'.

Your / You're

'Your' shows possession, as does 'our'.

> That is y**our** house and this is **our** house.

'You're' is short for you are.

> **You're** using an apostrophe in this sentence.

THE GRAMMAR ZONE

Getting your grammar spot on will help you make sure that you're writing and speaking clearly and properly. Use these memory tricks to help you get to grips with some of English grammar's trickier bits.

Nouns, Verbs, Adjectives and Adverbs

'Nouns', 'verbs', 'adjectives' and 'adverbs' are all very important when speaking and writing, but what exactly are they? Use the following memory tricks to help you remember them:

A **n**oun is a **n**aming word,
like 'ball' and 'bag' and 'bat' and 'bird'.

Verbs are commonly called 'doing words':

Vanishing, **E**ating, **R**unning and **B**urping
are all examples of **VERB**s!

An adjective is a word that describes a noun. If you think something is 'pretty', 'stinky', 'old' or 'scary', you're using an adjective every time. Remember:

An **ad**jective **ad**ds description to something.

Adverbs are like adjectives, but they describe verbs. So, if you talk about someone vanishing 'mysteriously', eating 'messily', running 'quickly' or burping 'loudly', you're using adverbs.

An **adverb** **ad**ds description to a **verb**.

Sentences

Every sentence you say or write is built using different parts.

A sentence can be made of one word or many words, but it must make sense by itself.

It has to have a verb – a doing word – and most sentences also have a subject – the person or thing that is doing the doing! Many sentences have an object, too – the person or thing that the doing is being done to.

To make sure you don't forget which is which, remember:

The **subject** hit the **object**.

Clauses and Phrases

Some sentences include 'clauses' and 'phrases'. The following sentence will help you to remember the difference between the two:

He loved **clauses**, but not **phrases**.

'He loved clauses' is a clause, because it has a subject ('he') and a verb ('loved').

'But not phrases' is a phrase because it doesn't have a subject and a verb, and does not make sense by itself.

Conjunctions

'Conjunctions' join phrases, clauses and sentences together, and there are three main types: co-ordinating, subordinate and correlative.

1. CO-ORDINATING CONJUNCTIONS
These are the words we use for joining similar things (such as two sentences) together. There are seven of them and a mnemonic used to remember them is **FAN BOYS**.

For, And, Nor, But, Or, Yet, So.

2. SUBORDINATE CONJUNCTIONS
'Subordinate conjunctions' join bits of a sentence that make sense on their own with bits that don't.

He tidied his room + **because** + he had to.

A mnemonic to remember common subordinate conjunctions is **BAT SWAB**.

Before, After, Though, So, While, As, Because.

3. CORRELATIVE CONJUNCTIONS
These are always found in pairs. An example of a pair of correlative conjunctions at work can be found in the sentence:

She liked **both** pink **and** red roses.

A mnemonic for common correlative conjunctions is
BEN and **ANN:**

> 'Both' goes with 'and'
> 'Either' goes with 'or'
> 'Neither' goes with 'nor'.

> 'As' goes with 'as'
> 'Not only' goes with 'but also'
> 'Not' goes with 'but'.

Prefixes and Suffixes

Words sometimes change their meaning or use when letters
are added to the beginning (prefixes) or the end (suffixes).

Prefixes usually change a word's meaning. You can
remember the common prefixes below by using the
mnemonic **DREAM**.

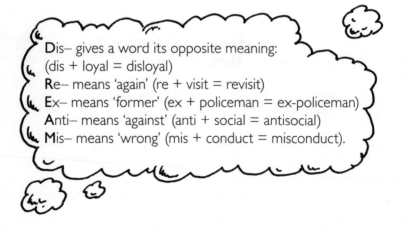

Dis– gives a word its opposite meaning:
(dis + loyal = disloyal)
Re– means 'again' (re + visit = revisit)
Ex– means 'former' (ex + policeman = ex-policeman)
Anti– means 'against' (anti + social = antisocial)
Mis– means 'wrong' (mis + conduct = misconduct).

Suffixes can either change a word's meaning – for example, 'use' + 'less' gives 'useless' – or how a word is used. For example, 'quick' + 'ly' changes the adjective 'quick' (a word describing a noun) to the adverb 'quickly' (a word describing a verb). Use the mnemonic **ICE TEA** to remember these common suffixes:

–**I**ze added to a noun creates a verb
(symbol + ize = symbolize)
–**C**y added to a verb, noun or adjective makes a noun
(urgent + cy = urgency)
–**E**ry added to a verb, noun or adjective makes a noun
(bake + ery = bakery)

–**T**ion added to a verb, noun or adjective makes a noun
(act + tion = action)
–**E**nt added to a verb or noun makes an adjective
(differ + ent = different)
–**A**ble added to a verb or noun makes an adjective
(drink + able = drinkable).

Verbs in the First, Second and Third Person

Verbs (doing words) can be written in the first, second or third person.

First person is used when the writer or speaker carries out the action: I run, we run. Second person is used when referring to 'you' in a sentence: you run. Third person is used when someone else is involved: he runs, she runs, it runs, they run.

👁 *Imagine you're waiting in line with a friend and his little brother for a go on a theme-park ride. You say, 'I will go **first**, **you** go **second** and **he** can go **third**.'*

WORD POWER!

Did you know that an impudent philatelist is just a cheeky stamp collector? No? Well, here are ten words you can remember and use to wow your teachers and your friends.

Acquiesce

To 'acquiesce' (pronounced ack–wee–ess) means to give in or to agree to something without complaining. Remember:

> I confess, I confess,
> I made the mess.
> So I'll clear it up.
> I **acquiesce**.

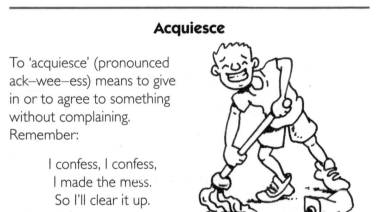

Chide

To 'chide' means to tell off or to scold.

> A teacher may **chide** a **chi**ld.

Claustrophobia

Words ending in **–phobia** describe a fear of something. 'Claustrophobia' means a fear of small, closed-in spaces.

> Santa **Claus** lives in the huge, open Arctic because he has **claus**trophobia.

Impudent

'Impudent' means cheeky or bold.

There's no creature so cheeky as an **imp**udent **imp**!

Myriad

'Myriad' means a very large number. Learn this short poem to help you remember the meaning.

Myriad friends will make you glad.
With so many friends you can't be sad!

Philatelist

A 'philatelist' is the name for a person who collects stamps.

👁 *Imagine you are making a record of all the stamps in your collection and have to **fill out a list.** ('Fill-out-a-list' sounds like 'philatelist'.)*

Quash

'Quash' means to forcefully stop an activity. Look at the example below:

The army s**quash**ed the rebellion.

Remembering that 'squashing a rebellion' and 'quashing a rebellion' mean the same will help you remember the meaning of 'quash'.

Serendipity

'Serendipity' is used to describe a lucky discovery. If you lose something and then find it when you aren't even looking for it, this is an example of serendipity.

>  *Imagine that you are playing hide-and-seek with your friend. While hiding in the cupboard, you find a long-lost toy and excitedly leave the cupboard to show your friend. Your friend thinks you are giving up and says:*
> *'Do you **surrender**? **Pity**!'*
> *('Surr-en-der-pit-y' sounds like 'ser-en-di-pit-y'.)*

Superlative

'Superlative' means outstanding or brilliant, as in: the sportsman made a superlative effort and won the gold medal. To help you with this word, remember that:

> **Super**man is not just a superhero, he's a **super**lative hero.

Taciturn

A 'taciturn' person is a person who is very quiet, and doesn't often join in conversations.

> I don't say much, I'm taciturn,
> So that's a word that I should learn.

GET JET SET!

A good memory is absolutely vital when learning a foreign language as there are so many new words to remember. The visualization exercises shown here take Spanish and French as examples, but you can use this technique to help you learn new words in any language you wish in a quick and fun way.

Spanish Words

The Spanish word for beach is *playa*. To remember this, carry out the following exercise:

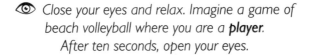 *Close your eyes and relax. Imagine a game of beach volleyball where you are a **player**. After ten seconds, open your eyes.*

Yes, it really is that easy! To prove it works, write the word beach on a piece of paper and leave it somewhere. Later in the day, look at your piece of paper with the word beach written on it. The image you created should come back to you and remind you that the Spanish word for beach is *playa*.

Here's another example to show how easy the visualization technique is. The Spanish word for hand is *mano*.

👁 *Close your eyes and imagine a tiny man standing on your hand. You are surprised to see him and exclaim, 'Oh!' in shock.*

Fixing this image in your mind will guarantee that you never forget that *mano* is the word for hand.

Here's one more example from Spanish, with a very silly visualization to help you remember it. The Spanish word for whale is *ballena*.

👁 *Imagine a huge whale dressed in a sparkly pink tutu, just like a **ballerina**.*

For trickier words like this, choosing a funny or crazy image to remember will help the word to stick in your mind more easily. Your ballet-dancing whale will make sure you always remember the Spanish word!

French Words

The French word for father is *père*. This is pronounced like the English word pear.

 *So, close your eyes and imagine your father eating a huge pear.*

The French word for apple is *pomme*.

This time imagine a cheerleader dancing at the side of a football pitch. However, instead of pompoms she is holding a giant apple in each hand.

The next time you go on holiday, or have language homework to do, try this technique and see how much easier it is to learn that vocabulary!

MATHS MASTER

MAKING MATHS ADD UP

Just the thought of maths is enough to terrify some people, especially when they are faced with complicated calculations. But using memory tricks to help you will soon simplify your sums and make maths less mean!

Tackling Tricky Sums

Using the acronym **BODMAS** will help you remember how to break down tricky sums and carry them out in the right order. Take this calculation, for example:

$$12 + 18 \div 6 \times (15 \div 5)^2 - 4$$

Order	Letter & Action	Calculation
1st	**B**rackets – carry out the calculation inside the brackets	$12 + 18 \div 6 \times (15 \div 5)^2 - 4$ becomes $12 + 18 \div 6 \times (3)^2 - 4$
2nd	**O**rder – this means the power, in this case the ^{2} sign	$12 + 18 \div 6 \times (3)^2 - 4$ becomes $12 + 18 \div 6 \times 9 - 4$
3rd	**D**ivision – work out any division calculations	$12 + 18 \div 6 \times 9 - 4$ becomes $12 + 3 \times 9 - 4$
4th	**M**ultiplication – work out any multiplication calculations	$12 + 3 \times 9 - 4$ becomes $12 + 27 - 4$
5th	**A**ddition – work out any addition calculations	$12 + 27 - 4$ becomes $39 - 4$
6th	**S**ubtraction – work out any subtraction calculations	$39 - 4 = 35$

NUMBER SMART

Find factors, sort square numbers and much more with these handy hints to help you become a true master of maths …

Prime Numbers

A 'prime number' is a number that can only be divided by itself and the number 1. You can remember this using:

I am pr**1**me because I can only be divided by **1** and **me**.

An easy way to work out your prime numbers is by using the following rules:

- 0 and 1 are not prime numbers and, apart from 2, no even numbers are prime.

- No numbers ending in 5 or 0 are prime, apart from 5.

- If the sum of a number's digits is divisible by 3, it's not a prime number.

Cardinal and Ordinal Numbers

'**C**ardinal numbers' are used for **c**ounting, so they tell you how many of something there are, such as 1 or 5.

'**Ord**inal numbers' tell you the **ord**er of things, such as 1st, 2nd or 3rd, for example.

Factors and Multiples

A whole number that divides into another whole number, with nothing left over, is known as a factor of that number. For example, 1, 2, 3 and 6 are all factors of 6.

A multiple of a number can be divided by that number, with no remainder. Some multiples of 6 include: 6, 12, 18 and 24.

Here's an easy way to remember them:

You **multipl**y to find a **multiple** and it's a **fact** that some numbers can be divided by many **fact**ors.

Square Numbers and Cube Numbers

A 'square number' is a number that's multiplied by itself. For example, 4^2, or 4 squared, means 4×4, which is 16. Remember this by picturing a square, which has two directions, and you'll remember that a square number has two numbers to multiply.

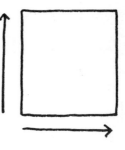

A cube has three directions, so

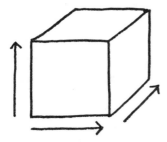

a 'cube number' has three numbers to multiply.

For example, 4^3, or 4 cubed, is $4 \times 4 \times 4$, which is 64.

Rounding Numbers

To round a decimal number to the nearest whole number, check the first number to the right of the decimal point. If it is five or more, round up. If it is less than five, round down. So, 4.7 would be rounded up to 5.

👁 *Imagine your maths teacher giving you a high-five for being a clever clogs!*

Co-ordinates

When you are plotting a graph, you use numbers called co-ordinates – such as (2,4) – to tell you where to position the next point. But should you move along the X-axis or the Y-axis first? You can remember with these simple reminders:

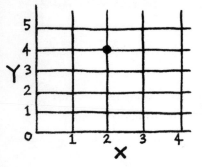

- The **X** co-ordinate is written first, and the **Y** co-ordinate second. Remember that **X** comes before **Y** in the alphabet to help you with this.

- On a graph, the X-axis is horizontal and the Y-axis is vertical. **X** is **a cross**, and it goes **across** the page.

- So in the above example, (2,4) means two spaces across on the X-axis and four spaces up the Y-axis.

Fabulous Fractions

A fraction represents part of a whole. Examples of common fractions you might come across are a half (½) or a quarter (¼).

Fractions are made up of two numbers. The 'denominator' is the number on the bottom. This tells you how many bits the whole number has been split into. The 'numerator', is the number on the top. This tells you how many parts of the number you're dealing with. For example, with ¼, the 4 lets you know that the whole has been divided into four bits, and the 1 tells you that you have one of those four bits.

To remember which is the numerator and which is the denominator in a fraction, use:

Numerator **up**, **d**enominator **d**own.

Dividing with Fractions

A calculation that involves a fraction might look scary, but there's an easy way to simplify it.

Take, for example, the sum 10 ÷ ¼. Use this little rhyme to help you:

Take the number you're dividing by,
Turn it upside-down and multiply.

So, 10 ÷ ¼ becomes 10 × 4⁄1
10 × 4⁄1 = 40, so 10 ÷ ¼ = 40

Averages

Do you know when to use the 'mean', 'mode' or 'median'?
Each one means something different in mathematics.

MEDIAN IN THE MIDDLE
The median is the middle number when a series of
numbers is put in order. So, for example, in this series the
median is seven:

4, 6, **7**, 9, 9

MOSTLY THE MODE
The **mo**de is the number that occurs **mo**st often. So in this
series, the mode is nine:

7, **9**, 4, 6, **9**

AVERAGELY MEAN
The mean is the average number. To work this out add the
numbers to find the total, and then divide the total by how
many numbers there are to get the average. For example:

$7 + 9 + 4 + 6 + 9 = 35$
There are five numbers, so $35 \div 5 = 7$

Still not clear? This little rhyme will help you remember:

Middle median, mostly mode
A **mean** old **add**er,
And a big green toad.

SHAPE UP

A two-dimensional shape (2-D), such as a square or a circle, is flat. It has two measurements: length and width. A three-dimensional shape (3-D), such as a cube or a sphere, has three measurements: length, width and depth. But do you know your parallelograms from your pyramids?

2-D Shapes

A **parallel**logram has opposite sides which are **parallel**, like railway tracks.

A **trap**ezoid has two parallel sides and two that, if they carried on going, would eventually crash into one another and become **trap**ped.

'Penta' comes from the Greek, meaning five. The word **'penta'** has five letters in it and a **penta**gon has five sides **on** it. A h**ex**agon has an **ex**tra one.

An **oct**agon has eight sides – just as an **oct**opus has eight tentacles.

3-D shapes

The Earth is a **sphere,** and so is the atmo**sphere** surrounding it.

A 'cylinder' is a tube with two circles of the same size at either end. Picture a can of soup to remember this shape.

A **cone** has a round or oval base and narrows to a point, like an ice-cream **cone**.

A **pyramid** has four triangular sides that meet at a point. The base is usually square, like the **Pyramids** of Egypt.

A **cube** has six square sides. This means the length, width and depth are all the same. To remember this shape, think of a sugar **cube**.

Easy as Pi

Pi, when spelt without an 'e', is a very important number in maths, not a tasty thing to eat for tea. Its symbol looks like this: π. It's especially useful when dealing with calculations to do with circles.

Usually, pi is shown as 3.14. But this is a number that has been rounded to two decimal places (see page 40 for more on rounding). In reality, the numbers after the decimal point go on infinitely. Why not impress your maths teacher by remembering pi to 21 decimal places? Use this sentence:

How I wish I could calculate pi. People would buy giant presents – sparkling diamond offerings – for me. How terrific it'll always be!

How does this strange saying work? Count the letters in each word in the sentence and you will have the answer:

3.141592653589793238462

Circumference, Radius and Diameter

Circle measurements may seem complicated, but they're easy to recall with these tips:

'Diameter' is a longer word than 'radius'. This will help you to remember that the diameter is the longer distance.

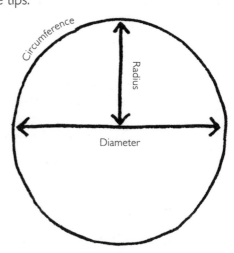

The 'circumference' is the distance around the circle. Think of the **circ**umference as a **circ**uit around a **circ**le. You can work out the circumference using pi.

The circumference of a circle is pi multiplied by the diameter.

This simple sentence will help you to remember the formula:

I was **pied** (π**D**) at the **circu**s.

Access All Areas

Imagine a room. The 'area' is the space occupied by a two-dimensional shape, such as the floor. Use this rhyme to help you find the area of a square, rectangle, triangle or circle:

> For a rectangle or a square
> Use length times width and you are there.
> For a triangle it's base times height,
> Put ½ in front to get it right.
> Circles are tricky, but don't be scared
> It's just pi (π) times the radius, squared.

Va Va Volume

Imagine a room again. The 'volume' is the space inside a three-dimensional shape, or the air inside the room.

If you know how to calculate the area of squares and circles, working out the volume of cubes and cylinders is easy.

Volume **E**quals (=) **A**rea × **D**epth

or

Violent **E**agles **A**re **D**angerous.

MARVELLOUS MEASUREMENTS

Units of Measurement

The metric system has seven base units or 'SI units' that measure different things:

Time is measured in seconds.
Temperature is measured in kelvins.
Length is measured in metres.
Current is measured in amperes.
Light is measured in candelas.
Amount is measured in moles.

You can remember these units using the following handy little story:

Mary the mole-catcher visited a **second** *time*. **Kelvin** waited in the *heat* at *length* to **meet her** (metre). There was no *current* for the **lamp** so he used **candle** *light* as he hunted the large *amount* of **moles**.

Quick Conversions

Most of Europe uses the metric system (metres, kilometres) to measure length. The United States mainly uses the imperial system (feet, miles). Some countries, like the United Kingdom, use both!

1 mile = 1.6093 kilometres (km), which can be rounded to 1.6 km. The easiest way to recall this is by remembering this little rhyme:

> Miles to kilometres, ain't it great,
> Just divide by 5 and times by 8.

1 inch = 2.54 centimetres (cm), which can be rounded to 2.5 cm. To remember this ratio, look at your school ruler.

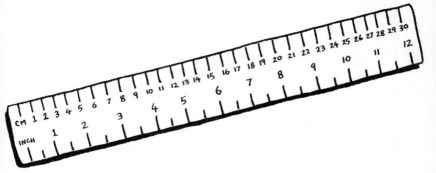

Most rulers are marked up to 12 inches on one side and 30 centimetres on the other.

$$12 \times 2.5 = 30$$

A GEOGRAPHICAL JOURNEY

PLANET POWER!

How much do you know about our amazing planet? This section will help you remember fascinating facts about Earth.

Inside the Planet

Planet Earth is divided into sections. If you were to dig deep down underground, you would pass through some very different layers.

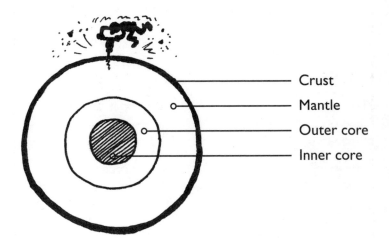

Crust

Mantle

Outer core

Inner core

Crust. You are standing on this layer right now. It's made of tectonic plates that move around, sometimes resulting in earthquakes. The crust is made of rock and it can be up to 70 km thick.

Mantle. This layer is nearly 3,000 km thick and is made of semi-molten rock. The closer to the centre of the Earth, the hotter and softer the rock becomes.

Core. The Earth's core is split into two – the outer core, and the inner core. The outer core is 2,300 km thick and is made of liquid iron and nickel, while the inner core is mainly solid iron and about 1,200 km thick. The inner core is incredibly hot, reaching temperatures of well over 5,000 degrees Celsius.

You can remember the four layers as follows:

> There's the **inner** and the **outer core**
> Then the **mantle** and the **crust** make four.

Our Atmosphere

The layer of gases that surrounds Earth is called the atmosphere. All planets have an atmosphere, but the gases they contain vary greatly.

The common name for Earth's atmosphere is 'air', and it's made up of different gases. About 78% is made up of a gas called nitrogen, 21% is oxygen, and the remaining 1% is argon.

You can remember the three most common gases in air in order (nitrogen, oxygen and argon) by using the sentence:

> Last **ni**ght, my smelly s**ox** (socks) caused an **arg**ument, and created a bad **atmosphere**.

Superb Spheres

The atmosphere changes as you move further away from the surface of Earth. The higher you go, the thinner the atmosphere becomes, until it eventually merges with space.

Scientists have given different names to various parts of the atmosphere, which they call 'spheres'. There are five of these:

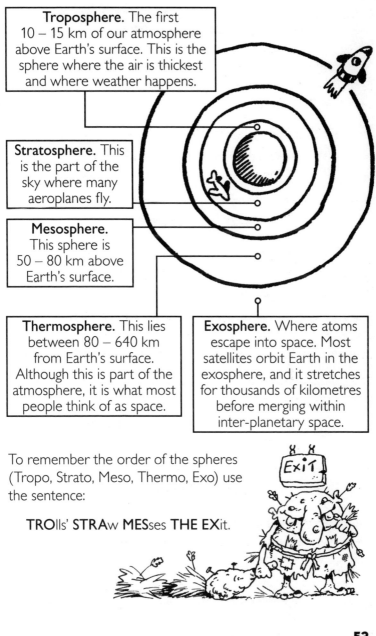

Troposphere. The first 10 – 15 km of our atmosphere above Earth's surface. This is the sphere where the air is thickest and where weather happens.

Stratosphere. This is the part of the sky where many aeroplanes fly.

Mesosphere. This sphere is 50 – 80 km above Earth's surface.

Thermosphere. This lies between 80 – 640 km from Earth's surface. Although this is part of the atmosphere, it is what most people think of as space.

Exosphere. Where atoms escape into space. Most satellites orbit Earth in the exosphere, and it stretches for thousands of kilometres before merging within inter-planetary space.

To remember the order of the spheres (Tropo, Strato, Meso, Thermo, Exo) use the sentence:

TROlls' **STRA**w **MES**ses **THE EX**it.

Sunrise, Sunset

Every day, it looks as though the Sun is moving across the sky. In fact, it's you, here on the Earth, who is moving. The Earth turns towards the east, so it seems as though the Sun is rising in the east, as your part of the Earth turns towards it, and then setting in the west, as your part of the Earth turns away from it and night falls. To remember this, use the sentence:

> The Sun rises **ea**rly in the **ea**st and sets in the **we**st when it is **we**ary.

Arctic / Antarctic

The coldest places on Earth are the polar regions – huge ice-covered areas surrounding the North and South Poles.

The North Pole is found, as its name suggests, at the most northerly part of the planet, and the polar region there is called the Arctic. The South Pole lies at the most southerly part of Earth, and the polar region there is called the Antarctic.

To avoid confusing the two areas, notice that the only difference in the names is that one has the letters 'Ant' in front of 'Arctic'. To remember that the **Ant**arctic is in the south:

👁 *Imagine a little **ant** heading south for his holidays.*

You probably already know that polar bears and penguins live at the poles. It might surprise you to learn that no polar bear has ever eaten a penguin. This is because polar bears live in the Arctic, and penguins live in the Antarctic. To remember that **pen**guins live in the **Ant**arctic:

👁 *Imagine your holidaying **ant** writing a postcard with a **pen**.*

Magma and Lava

Deep inside the Earth, the temperature is so hot that the rocks melt. This hot, liquid rock is called magma. Sometimes, this magma escapes to the surface when a volcano erupts. When the liquid rock is on the surface of the Earth, it is called lava. In other words, magma and lava are used to describe the same substance in different places. Many people confuse the two words but, remember:

Lava is on **la**nd.

Hurricanes, Typhoons and Cyclones

The names of strong circular storms with very high winds that begin over warm seas vary depending on where they are found. When the storms occur in the Atlantic Ocean, they are called hurricanes, when they happen in the Pacific Ocean, they are called typhoons, and in the Indian Ocean, they are called cyclones.

So: Hurricane = Atlantic, Cyclone = Indian, Typhoon = Pacific.

This mnemonic will help you to remember what happens where:

> Mr **A. T. Lant**ic **hurr**ied as he **cycl**ed to **India**,
> but he grew **ti**red by the **pac**e.

Sorting Out Those Scales

Richter Scale. This scale is used to calculate the power of earthquakes. It is an unusual scale as it increases by powers of ten. This means a quake measuring six on the scale is ten times more powerful than one measuring five! To remember the name of this scale:

👁 *Imagine a king losing all his **rich**es in an earthquake.*

Beaufort Scale. This is used to measure wind speed. 0 is calm weather, and the scale continues to 12, which means hurricane conditions with wind speeds above 118 km/hour.

> 👁 *Imagine someone trying to tie a **bow** to
> the top of a **fort**ress in the wind.*

Saffir / Simpson Scale. Once a wind becomes a hurricane, it moves beyond the Beaufort Scale and is measured by the Saffir / Simpson Scale. This goes from one to five. The most famous hurricane in recent history was Hurricane Katrina – a Category Four hurricane that caused terrible damage to the city of New Orleans in 2005.

👁 *Imagine a ship called the* **SS Hurricane** *on a stormy sea.*

Fujita Scale. This scale measures tornadoes, which can have wind speeds even faster than hurricanes! This scale goes from EF0 (up to 135 km/hour) to EF5 (over 320 km/hour). Visualizing something silly can help you remember this.

👁 *Imagine a man being swept up in a tornado while eating* **fudge**. *('Fudge-eater' sounds like 'Fujita'.)*

Tricky Temperatures

There are two different ways of measuring the temperature – in degrees Celsius, or in degrees Fahrenheit. The two scales are quite different, but you can use these two little rhymes to help you remember the difference between them:

Celsius	**Fahrenheit**
30 is hot,	32's freezing,
20 is nice,	50 is not,
10 is chilly,	68's pleasant,
0 is ice!	85's hot!

The Water Cycle

Water is vital for life on Earth. It doesn't run out because it is in constant motion – from the land, to the seas and rivers, to the sky and back to the land.

As it makes this journey, water changes from a liquid to a gas and back again (sometimes, it also becomes a solid when it turns to ice).

This continual movement of the Earth's water is called the water cycle. The stages of the cycle are shown in the diagram below.

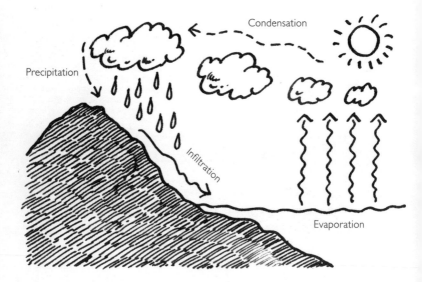

Don't worry if this diagram looks complicated – read on to find out more about each of the different stages of the water cycle and how you can remember them.

Evaporation.
'Evaporation' changes water into gas (this is why puddles disappear when the Sun comes out after rain).

Precipitation.
'Precipitation' is a fancy word for any sort of water that falls from the sky, after it's been condensed. Rain, snow, hail and even mist are all forms of precipitation.

Condensation.
'Condensation' changes a gas to a liquid. This process forms water droplets and creates clouds.

Infiltration.
'Infiltration' happens when the rain hits the ground. Sometimes it soaks into it, and sometimes it runs off the surface and into rivers and lakes.

This poem will help you to remember the four stages and what happens in each:

Evaporation turns water into **vap**our, a gas floating on high,
Condensation makes it **dens**er, clouds appear in the sky,
Precipitation falls as rain that you can **sip**,
Then in**fil**tration **fil**ls up lakes and trickles drip by drip.

59

Cloudspotting

If you want to take up a new hobby, why don't you try cloudspotting? It's very easy, as all you have to do is find a comfortable bit of grass, lie down and stare up at the sky. If anyone accuses you of being lazy, you can truthfully tell them that you are actually very busy cloudspotting. This picture shows the main types of cloud to look out for.

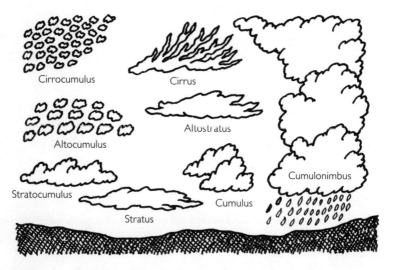

The names used to describe clouds can seem confusing at first, but there are clues to help you tell which is which. The first way of distinguishing clouds is by height. Use **CASE** to help you remember in 'case' you see a cloud.

Cirrus is used for high clouds.
Alto describes clouds at middle height.
Stratus is used to describe low clouds.
Earth is where you're lying looking up at the clouds!

Other words to describe clouds are:

Cumulus. White, puffy clouds that looks like cotton wool:
CUMulus = **COM**fy cotton wool.

Stratus. Flat clouds spread out straight across the sky:
STRatus = **STR**aight.

Nimbus. Rain clouds:
You need to run **NIMB**ly to avoid rain from these
NIMBus clouds.

If you remember these terms, you will be able to decode
many different cloud types and impress people! For example:

Cirrocumulus = cirrus + cumulus = high, puffy cloud

Altostratus = alto + stratus = mid-height, flat cloud.

Most Active Volcanoes

There are more than 1,500 volcanoes on land that have
erupted in the last 10,000 years. Some of the most active
volcanoes have been continuously erupting for hundreds
of years.

The three most active
volcanoes are: **M**ount **E**tna (in
Sicily), **S**tromboli (on the Aeolian
Islands off the coast of Italy), and
Yasur (on the island of Vanuatu
in the South Pacific). To recall
these three, remember:

Mum **E**ats **S**melly **Y**ogurts!

ALL AROUND THE WORLD

A Capital Memory

Turning a list of information into a story can really help your memory. You're about to read about George and his car trip, but you'll actually learn all the capital cities of South America! Start in Guyana and travel anticlockwise, then get ready to impress your friends with your slick city knowledge.

One day, **George** (**George**town) got in his **car** (**Car**acas) and drove through a **bog** (**Bog**otá) without **quit**ting (**Quit**o). He put his pet **lemur** (**Lim**a) on his **lap** (**La P**az); the one he got from **Santa** (**Sant**iago). He wound down the window for some fresh **air** (Buenos **Air**es), then stopped to make a **video** (Monte**video**) of a man and **a son** (**Asun**ción). Then he had a little picnic of a **brazil** (**Brasil**ia) nut with **cayenne** (**Cayenne**) pepper, which is where this **para**graph (**Para**maribo) ends.

Bogotá, Colombia

Caracas, Venezuela

Georgetown, Guyana

Paramaribo, Suriname

Cayenn French G

Quito, Equador

Lima, Peru

Brasilia, Brazil

La Paz, Bolivia

Asunción, Paraguay

Montevide Uruguay

Buenos Aires, Argentina

Santiago, Chile

Island Information

As well as its seven continents, the world is full of islands. Some of these are enormous – much bigger than many countries. With just a couple of silly sentences in your head, you'll be able to remember the five biggest islands in the world, as well as all the islands in the Mediterranean Sea.

The five biggest islands in the world each have a landmass of more than half-a-million square kilometres. In size order, these are:

Greenland, **New Guinea,**
Borneo, Madaga**scar**
and Ba**ffin**.

Have a look on a map of the world and see if you can spot them all. To remember these five supersized islands, think about this sentence:

My **green new guinea**-pig was **born** with a **scar** shaped like a pu**ffin**.

Now it's time for some Mediterranean sunshine. Here are the main islands of the Mediterranean Sea, in order from the west (near Spain) to the east (near Turkey): **Bal**earic Islands, **Sardin**ia, **Cors**ica, Si**cily**, **Crete**, **Cyp**rus.

Or:

Balloons in **sardin**es **cause** si**lly crate**s of **soup.**

States and State Capitals

Trying to remember the 50 states of America and each of their capital cities might seem like an impossible task. But, by using a combination of memory tricks, your brilliant brain will tackle it in no time.

First, use the grouping technique to put the 50 states into five chunks of ten, in alphabetical order. Then, using some of those silly sentences, add in the information about each state capital.

Group One:

STATE	CAPITAL
Alabama	**M**ontgomery
Alaska	**J**uneau
Arizona	**P**hoenix
Arkansas	**L**ittle Rock
California	**S**acramento
Colorado	**D**enver
Connecticut	**H**artford
Delaware	**D**over
Florida	**T**allahassee
Georgia	**A**tlanta

To remember these first ten state capitals, use the silly sentence:

My **J**umping **P**ony Likes Shouting, 'Delicious **H**ot **D**oughnuts!' **T**otally **A**mazing!

Group Two:

STATE	CAPITAL
Hawaii	Honolulu
Idaho	Boise
Illinois	Springfield
Indiana	Indianapolis
Iowa	Des Moines
Kansas	Topeka
Kentucky	Frankfort
Louisiana	Baton Rouge
Maine	Augusta
Maryland	Annapolis

Remember:

How Big Should I Decide To Finally Build An Ark?

Group Three:

STATE	CAPITAL
Massachusetts	Boston
Michigan	Lansing
Minnesota	St. Paul
Mississippi	Jackson
Missouri	Jefferson City
Montana	Helena
Nebraska	Lincoln
Nevada	Carson City
New Hampshire	Concord
New Jersey	Trenton

Remember:

Beautiful Ladies Slurp Juicy Jellies Happily, Looking Completely Cool, Too!

Group Four:

STATE	CAPITAL
New Mexico	**S**anta Fe
New York	**A**lbany
North Carolina	**R**aleigh
North Dakota	**B**ismarck
Ohio	**C**olumbus
Oklahoma	**O**klahoma City
Oregon	**S**alem
Pennsylvania	**H**arrisburg
Rhode Island	**P**rovidence
South Carolina	**C**olumbia

Remember:

Serious **A**nimals **R**ead
Books '**C**os **O**ther **S**illy
Happy **P**eople **C**an't.

Group Five:

STATE	CAPITAL
South Dakota	**P**ierre
Tennessee	**N**ashville
Texas	**A**ustin
Utah	**S**alt Lake City
Vermont	**M**ontpelier
Virginia	**R**ichmond
Washington	**O**lympia
West Virginia	**C**harleston
Wisconsin	**M**adison
Wyoming	**C**heyenne

Remember:

Paul's **N**ephew **A**ndrew **S**pilt **M**ilk **R**ight
On **C**harlie's **M**um's **C**at!

Money Money Money!

Money makes the world go round, but not every country uses the same sort of money, or 'currency'. There are actually over 180 different currencies in existence throughout the world.

Don't get your pesos in a pickle or your dollars in a dilemma! Here's a quick mnemonic for the currencies of a dozen different countries:

Just remember that a **CUP** of **chilly pesos** costs **JUST** a **dollar** or **A BIG euro**.

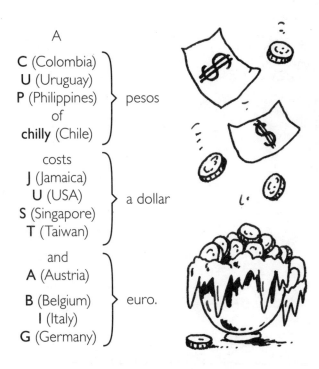

A

C (Colombia)
U (Uruguay)
P (Philippines) ⎬ pesos
of
chilly (Chile)

costs
J (Jamaica)
U (USA) ⎬ a dollar
S (Singapore)
T (Taiwan)

and
A (Austria)
B (Belgium) ⎬ euro.
I (Italy)
G (Germany)

THE LIVING WORLD

LIVING ORGANISMS

There are billions of living things crawling all over the planet. These are known as organisms. This section will help you to remember all sorts of cool stuff about animals and plants, as well as your fellow human beings.

Cool Characteristics

Living organisms can be as different as an elephant and a daffodil. However, there are seven characteristics shared by all living things. Look at the first letters of the list below, and you will see how **MRS GREN** will help you remember these:

Movement. All living things move. Plants with roots move their leaves towards the Sun.

Respiration. This is the name given to the process where living organisms release energy from the food they consume.

Sensitivity. All living organisms can sense certain things in their environment that affect them (such as light) and respond to them.

Growth. All living things grow.

Reproduction. All living organisms reproduce in order to continue the species.

Excretion. Living things get rid of waste products. You do this by going to the toilet.

Nutrition. Living organisms need to take in energy, usually by eating and drinking for animals, and photosynthesis for plants (see page 72).

POTTY ABOUT PLANTS

Parts of a Flower

Flowers come in all sizes and colours, but did you know that all flowers are made up of different parts?

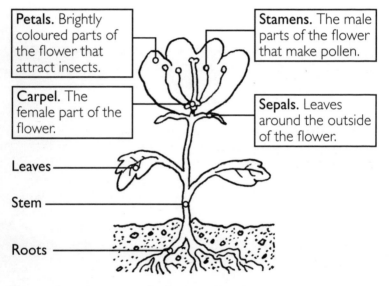

Petals. Brightly coloured parts of the flower that attract insects.

Carpel. The female part of the flower.

Stamens. The male parts of the flower that make pollen.

Sepals. Leaves around the outside of the flower.

Leaves

Stem

Roots

Remember the parts of a flower using the sentence:

See (sepal) your **pet** (petal) **sta**nding (stamen) on the **carpe**t (carpel).

All flowers are plants, but not all plants are flowers. The three parts that all plants have are:

Stem. This structure helps the plant to grow and spread its leaves, and moves water and nutrients from the roots to the leaves.

Leaves. Green leaves capture energy from sunlight.

Roots. These absorb water and nutrients from the soil. They also hold the plant in place. Remember:

Starving **L**ions **R**oar!

Tree Types

There are two main types of tree:

Deciduous trees. These shed their leaves in the autumn and remain bare until the next growing season.

I **decid**e to **leave** in the autumn.

Coniferous trees. These include pines and firs. Their leaves, which are like thin needles, are not shed. They are usually called evergreen trees or conifers.

It's a big **con** if **fir**s shed leaves because they're supposed to be evergreen.

Plant Growth

Plants need four things in order to grow. These are known as the **SWAN**:

Sunlight
Water
Air
Nutrients.

Photosynthesis

The mnemonic **SWAN** on page 71 reminds you what plants need for 'photosynthesis', the process where green leaves convert sunlight, carbon dioxide and water into sugar that helps the plant to grow. To remember this process, remember this rhyme:

> The plant takes carbon dioxide and water.
> And then the Sun shines just like it oughta!
> This turns them to sugar, the plant's favourite food
> And oxygen too, which it kicks out … how rude!

ANIMAL MAD

You Are What You Eat

Animals are divided into groups based on what they eat.

Herbivores. These animals only eat plants. Notice that the word **herb**ivore begins with 'herb'. This will help you remember that these animals are plant-eaters.

Carnivores. 'Carnivores' are meat-eaters. They get their meat by eating other animals. The Spanish word for meat is *carne*. If you eat the dish *chilli con carne*, you are eating chilli with meat. So **carn**ivore means meat-eater.

Omnivores. 'Omnivores' eat plants and meat. Humans – unless they are vegetarians – are omnivores. So **om**nivores will happily eat a ham and spinach **om**elette.

Vertebrates and Invertebrates

Another way to classify animals is as either 'vertebrates' or 'invertebrates'.

Invertebrates. These animals do not have a backbone. You might think there are not many of these, but invertebrates make up the vast majority of the world's creatures – from octopuses and spiders to crabs and bees.

Vertebrates. These are animals that have a backbone or spine, like you.

Vertebrates are divided into five classes: **B**irds, **F**ish, **A**mphibians, **R**eptiles and **M**ammals. Any animal that doesn't fit into these classes is an invertebrate.

You can remember the five classes of vertebrates by using the sentence:

Vertebrates must **B**e kept on a **FARM**.

Big Cats

There are lots of different species of wild cat, but only four of them are technically known as big cats. This classification actually has nothing to do with their size, but whether they can roar!

The true big cats are: leopards, lions, tigers and jaguars. To remember them, use the sentence:

Leo Likes **T**o **J**ump.

Marsupials

One group of mammals is known as marsupials. These animals give birth when their babies are not well-developed, so marsupials usually have pouches to keep their babies safe.

Many marsupials live in Australia The most famous marsupials are **w**allabies, **k**angaroos, **w**ombats and **k**oalas.

As these marsupials spend most of the day asleep, you can remember them by shouting, 'WaKey! WaKey!'

Insects

Four out of every five species on the planet are insects. Some of the most common insects you'll find crawling and scuttling about are: **bee**tles, **bee**s, butter**flies**, **flies** and **grass**hoppers.

This mnemonic will help you remember these five common groups:

Two **bee**s and two **flies** hopped on the **grass**.

THE BRILLIANT HUMAN BODY

The Truth About Teeth

Have you noticed that your teeth are different shapes and sizes?

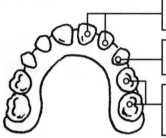

Incisors. These flat teeth help you bite into your food.

Canines. These are pointy teeth that help you tear food.

Molars. The thick teeth at the back of the mouth that are for grinding food.

To remember the three types of teeth, use the sentence:

My teeth bite **in**to (incisors) a **can** (canines) of **mola**sses (molars).

Feel It In Your Bones

You might hear people talking about the 'leg bone', but did you know that actually there's no such thing? In fact, your leg is made of four separate bones. These are the femur, the patella, the tibia and the fibula. To remember these, think about:

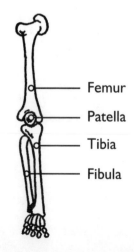

Femur

Patella

Tibia

Fibula

A **fem**ale (femur) called **Pat** (patella) and her twins, **Tib** (tibia) and **Fib** (fibula).

76

Veins, Arteries and Capillaries

The heart pumps blood around the body. The blood travels through vessels called arteries, capillaries and veins, which are like little pipes running through the body.

Arteries. These carry blood that has been pumped out of the heart and is full of oxygen.

Capillaries. These are very thin pipes, which allow the blood to release its oxygen through their walls into your body's tissue. Waste products are then sent back through the capillary wall and into the blood.

Veins. The veins take the blood back to the heart, ready for it to be refilled with oxygen.

> So, **a**rteries send blood **a**way from the heart,
> and **ve**ins re**ve**rse the direction.
> **Cap**illaries let oxygen es**cap**e through their walls.

Did you know?

If all the arteries, veins and capillaries were taken out of your body and laid out in a single line, it would stretch at least twice around the planet!

Making Sense of Senses

You take in information about the world around you with your senses. There are five of these: sight, smell, touch, taste and hearing.

To help you remember the five senses, just think of the five things on your face – eyes (sight), nose (smell), mouth (taste), ears (hearing) and skin (touch).

The Excellent Eyes

Your eyes are made up of several different parts, which all work together to help you see.

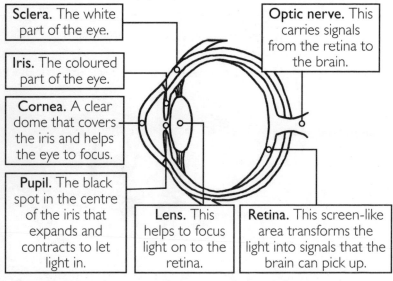

Sclera. The white part of the eye.

Iris. The coloured part of the eye.

Cornea. A clear dome that covers the iris and helps the eye to focus.

Pupil. The black spot in the centre of the iris that expands and contracts to let light in.

Optic nerve. This carries signals from the retina to the brain.

Lens. This helps to focus light on to the retina.

Retina. This screen-like area transforms the light into signals that the brain can pick up.

To remember the parts of your eye, (**s**clera, **i**ris, **c**ornea, **p**upil, **l**ens, **r**etina, **o**ptic **n**erve) use the sentence:

SICk Penguins Love iRONing!

The Internal Organs

The human body is a very complex organism.

Inside your body, a lot of different things that are essential for life are happening all the time. There are specialized body parts that handle these tasks. We call these body parts organs.

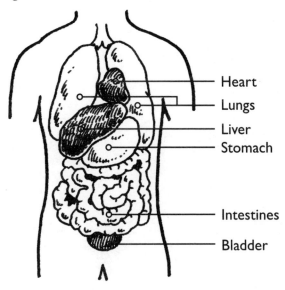

To help you remember what the internal organs do, learn this little rhyme:

Start with the **heart**, which pumps blood around inside,
Lungs take in oxygen and expel carbon dioxide.
The **liver** cares for the blood, removing the bad stuff,
The **stomach** digests your food for you, even when it's tough.
The **intestines** absorb food and get rid of the waste,
Then the **bladder** stores urine, so you don't pee in haste!

SUPER SCIENCE

GET SCIENCE SORTED

Science is a fascinating subject to study, but there are lots of things to remember, which can sometimes make it tricky. This section will help you to conquer your chemistry and finesse your physics. Read on to become a science superstar!

Science VIPs

Science has advanced so much over the centuries because of the amazing work and discoveries of some of history's most brilliant minds, from ancient Greece to modern times.

Use this little poem to remember some of the most famous scientists and their discoveries, and then read on to find out a bit more about them:

> The Greek **Archimedes** was a knowledge seeker,
> Thought up his Principle and yelled 'Eureka!'
> **Copernicus** told us Earth circles the Sun,
> While **Galileo's** weights both fell as one.
> **Newton's** law of gravity was more than a wish,
> And hydrogen was discovered by Mr **Cavendish**.
> **Darwin** talked of evolution when no one dared,
> And **Einstein** taught us that $E = mc^2$.

ARCHIMEDES (AROUND 287 – 212 BC)
Archimedes came up with the Archimedes Principle. This states that when an object is put in water, it loses as much weight as an equal volume of the water. Legend says that he discovered this while sitting in the bath and was so excited by his discovery that he leapt out and ran naked through the streets, shouting 'Eureka!'

Nicolaus Copernicus (1473 – 1543)

Copernicus was an astronomer who stated that the Earth travels around the Sun and that the Sun remains in the same place. This was a very new idea because at the time, people thought that the Earth lay at the centre of the universe.

Galileo Galilei (1564 – 1642)

Galileo was an Italian scientist who made a number of important discoveries. He found out that all objects fall at the same speed. To prove this, he climbed to the top of the Leaning Tower of Pisa and dropped two balls. Although one of the balls was very heavy and one was light, they both reached the ground at the same time.

Isaac Newton (1642 – 1727)

Isaac Newton is most famous for his theory of gravity. This states that there is a force between objects and that the size of the force depends on their mass and the distance between them. In one of the most famous legends in science, it is said that his ideas about gravity struck him at the same time as he was struck on the head by a falling apple while sitting under an apple tree.

HENRY CAVENDISH (1731 – 1810)

Henry Cavendish was a British scientist who spent his life studying science and discovered the gas hydrogen.

CHARLES DARWIN (1809 – 1882)

Charles Darwin spent years sailing around the world studying the animals and plants he found. This provided him with much of the knowledge and information he needed for his book, *On The Origin Of Species,* which explained his theories about how living organisms change over time to adapt to their environment.

ALBERT EINSTEIN (1879 – 1955)

Albert Einstein was the most famous scientist of the last century. He made huge contributions to physics, such as proving that atoms exist, but he is most famous for his theory of relativity. His ideas are very complicated, but this theory gave an explanation of light, distance, mass and energy. One of the results of his theories was his discovery that the energy in an object can be calculated by multiplying the mass of the object by the speed of light squared. This is written as:

$$E = mc^2 \text{ (Energy = mass} \times \text{ speed of light}^2)$$

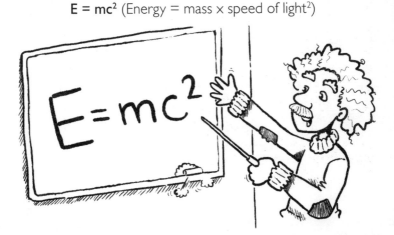

What Makes a Metal?

Metals are very useful in all parts of our lives. They are used for making a wide range of objects – from enormous bridges and powerful machines to beautiful pieces of jewellery and the tiniest of computer parts.

Most metals share the following characteristics:

- Shiny appearance
- Strength
- Solid at room temperature
- High melting-point
- Good conductor of electricity and heat
- Malleable – this means it can be beaten into different shapes without breaking.

This short poem will help you remember the key properties of metals:

They're **shiny**, **strong** and **solid**.
They **conduct** and they are **malleable**.
They do not **melt** easily,
That's why they are so valuable!

Marvellous Magnets

Magnetism is an invisible force that causes objects to attract each other. A magnet is an object that gives off a magnetic field. This means it applies a force over a distance that will attract anything made of iron.

Every magnet has two ends called the north pole (N) and the south pole (S). These are the magnetic poles.

If you put two magnets next to each other, they can either attract each other (where they snap together) or repel each other (where they push each other away). The rule is that:

Opposite poles attract and similar poles repel.

If you have two magnets, try this for yourself.

There is a saying that when it comes to romance, opposites attract. A loud person is likely to fall in love with a quiet person, for example.

Magnets may not be as romantic, but the rule of 'opposites attract' can help you remember which poles attract and which repel.

ALL ABOUT ENERGY

Every time you turn on a light, run hot water or travel in a car, you are using energy resources. Most of this energy comes from fossil fuels. However, as the world's energy demands grow, it has become important to find new sources of energy, especially renewable ones that will not run out.

Fossil Fuels

The fossil fuels are coal, oil and gas. They are called fossil fuels because they have formed over millions of years from

the remains of prehistoric plants and animals.

To remember these three fuels, think of fossil fuel energy being used to power the turning of a **COG**:

Coal **O**il **G**as.

There are two ways to use this fuel. Sometimes, the fuels are used directly when people burn coal for heat, or use gas for cooking and oil to power engines. However, most of our energy comes from power stations, where the fuels are burned to create electricity. This process goes like this:

Burn fuel to heat water and make steam.	→	The steam makes a turbine turn.	→	The turbine turns a generator.	→	The generator creates electricity.

To remember each **STaGE** in the process, remember:

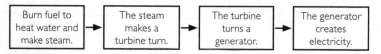

Steam **T**urbine **a** **G**enerator **E**lectricity.

Renewable Energy

When we use fossil fuels, the source is used up forever. Renewable energy sources can be used again and again without running out. These include: wind farms, wave power stations, biofuel power stations (which burn solid waste instead of fossil fuels), geo-thermal energy (which uses the heat from inside the Earth), hydro-electric power stations (which use dams to channel water through tunnels) and solar energy from the Sun.

Remember these six renewable energy sources (**w**ind, **wa**ve, **b**iofuels, **g**eo-thermal, **h**ydro-electric and **s**olar) by asking the question:

Why **Wa**ste **B**rilliantly **G**ood **H**eat **S**ources?

Kinetic and Potential Energy

Energy when it's in motion is called kinetic energy. For example, a big boulder rolling down a hill has lots of kinetic energy because it's on the move.

Energy that's stored or waiting to happen is called potential energy. When the boulder is sitting at the top of the hill, it's full of potential energy. Remember:

It's **kin**etic when it's **in** motion, and **p**otential when it's on **p**ause.

The Electromagnetic Spectrum

Energy often travels from one place to another in waves of charged particles. This is called electromagnetic radiation. Different types of waves have different wavelengths.

When the different electromagnetic wavelengths are positioned in order from the longest waves to the shortest waves, this is called the electromagnetic spectrum.

Visible light is part of this spectrum, and it's the only type of electromagnetic wave that your eyes can see. Visible light waves are split up into the colours of the rainbow, with red waves the longest and violet waves the shortest. When all the coloured waves are seen together, they make bright, white light.

The spectrum in full, going from the longest wave to the shortest wave, looks like this: **r**adio waves, **m**icrowaves, **i**nfrared, **v**isible **l**ight (**r**ed, **o**range, **y**ellow, **g**reen, **b**lue, **i**ndigo, **v**iolet), **u**ltraviolet, **x**-rays, **g**amma radiation.

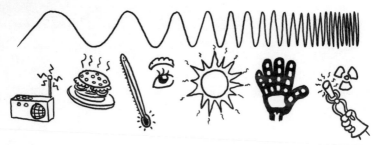

To remember the full spectrum, try using the silly sentence:

Rich **M**en **I**nflate **V**egetables **L**ovingly (**Re**ally **O**ld **Y**ucky **G**reen **B**eans **I**ncite **Viole**nce) **U**sing **X**ylophones. **G**reat!

THE PERIODIC TABLE

Everything you can see around you, including yourself, is made of elements. These elements are the building blocks of the whole universe.

The elements are organized using the periodic table, which is shown below. This looks complicated at first glance, but is easy to follow once you know how it is arranged.

It's Elementary ...

1 H																	2 He
3 Li	4 Be											5 B	6 C	7 N	8 O	9 F	10 Ne
11 Na	12 Mg											13 Al	14 Si	15 P	16 S	17 Cl	18 Ar
19 K	20 Ca	21 Sc	22 Ti	23 V	24 Cr	25 Mn	26 Fe	27 Co	28 Ni	29 Cu	30 Zn	31 Ga	32 Ge	33 As	34 Se	35 Br	36 Kr
37 Rb	38 Sr	39 Y	40 Zr	41 Nb	42 Mo	43 Tc	44 Ru	45 Rh	46 Pd	47 Ag	48 Cd	49 In	50 Sn	51 Sb	52 Te	53 I	54 Xe
55 Cs	56 Ba	57 - 71 La-Lu	72 Hf	73 Ta	74 W	75 Re	76 Os	77 Ir	78 Pt	79 Au	80 Hg	81 Tl	82 Pb	83 Bi	84 Po	85 At	86 Rn
87 Fr	88 Ra	89 - 103 Ac-Lr	104 Rf	105 Db	106 Sg	107 Bh	108 Hs	109 Mt	110 Uun	111 Uuu	112 Uub	113 Uut	114 Uuq	115 Uup	116 Uuh	117 Uus	118 Uuo

57 La	58 Ce	59 Pr	60 Nd	61 Pm	62 Sm	63 Eu	64 Gd	65 Tb	66 Dy	67 Ho	68 Er	69 Tm	70 Yb	71 Lu
89 Ac	90 Th	91 Pa	92 U	93 Np	94 Pu	95 Am	96 Cm	97 Bk	98 Cf	99 Es	100 Fm	101 Md	102 No	103 Lr

The periodic table is organized into periods and groups. The periods go across the periodic table in rows, and the groups go down the table in columns.

Each element is represented on the periodic table by a symbol. Sometimes, this is part of its name (**Li**thium is represented by **Li**, for example), but just to be tricky, some of the symbols represent the Latin name of the element. For example, potassium is represented by the letter **K**, because its Latin name is **K**alium.

Try not to let these confuse you. The periodic table is the perfect place to come up with some really silly sentences and get those elements memorized! Here's an example for Group One on the table, which is made up of hydrogen (**H**) lithium (**Li**), sodium (**Na**), potassium (**K**), rubidium (**Rb**), caesium (**Cs**) and francium (**Fr**).

Horrid **Li**ttle **Na**talie **K**eeps **R**o**b**bing **C**atherine's **Fr**iends.

Now here's one for Group Two, which is made up of beryllium (**Be**), magnesium (**Mg**), calcium (**Ca**), strontium (**Sr**), barium (**Ba**) and radium (**Ra**).

Beginner **M**a**g**icians **Ca**n **Se**riously **Ba**ffle **Ra**bbits!

Have a go at creating some silly sentences of your own for the other groups of the periodic table.

Chemical Compounds

A chemical compound is made from at least two different chemical elements found in the periodic table (see page 89).

A famous example of a chemical compound is water, which has the formula H_2O. It is made from hydrogen (H) and oxygen (O), with two hydrogen atoms bonded to every oxygen atom. Compounds are organized into the following categories:

Acids. These react with other chemicals. A well-known acid is citric acid, which is found in fruits such as lemons.

Bases. A base is the opposite of an acid. Acids are measured on the pH scale. A compound with a pH above seven is a base, one with a pH below seven is an acid.

Salts. Bases and acids can sometimes react to make a salt. The salt you put on your food is called sodium chloride and has the formula NaCl (Na is the symbol for sodium and Cl is chlorine).

Oxides. Oxides are compounds of elements with oxygen. When iron (Fe) forms a compound with oxygen (O) it creates iron oxide, which is better known as 'rust' (Fe_2O_3).

Organic. An organic compound is one that contains carbon.

To remember these categories, it's time for a silly sentence:

Acid**ic B**ase**balls S**ave **Ox**en's **Organ**s.

HISTORY HELPER

REMEMBERING WHEN ...

History is packed with important dates and events. Learning them all may seem tricky, but these tips will help you to keep track of what happened when.

BC or AD?

Sometimes dates have letters next to them – AD, meaning *Anno Domini* (the Latin for 'year of our Lord') or BC, meaning 'Before Christ'. These letters divide time before and after when people thought Jesus Christ was born. Remember:

BC comes **b**efore, **A**D follows **a**fter.

First Things First ...

Early humans lived through three prehistoric ages: the **S**tone **A**ge, the **B**ronze **A**ge and the **I**ron **A**ge. To remember these in the right order, use the sentence:

Sarah **A**lways **B**eats **A**nna **I**n **A**rithmetic.

The study of ancient civilizations is fascinating. To remember that the **a**ncient **E**gyptians came before the **a**ncient **G**reeks, who came before the **a**ncient **R**omans, use the sentence:

Alice **E**ats **A**pples, **G**rapes **A**nd **R**aspberries.

Dinosaur Days

The dinosaurs roamed the Earth during three main geological periods – the Triassic, the Jurassic, and the Cretaceous.

TRIASSIC PERIOD (251 – 200 MILLION YEARS AGO)
During the Triassic Period, all the world's land formed one massive continent. The first dinosaurs evolved, along with pterosaurs – small flying reptiles.

In the **Tri**assic, a **tri**ckle of dinosaurs appear.

JURASSIC PERIOD (200 – 146 MILLION YEARS AGO)
In the Jurassic Period, the landmass began to break up into continents, and forests appeared. Larger dinosaurs, such as the diplodocus, stegosaurus and brachiosaurus evolved.

The **J**urassic **P**eriod is **j**am-**p**acked with big dinosaurs.

CRETACEOUS PERIOD (146 – 66 MILLION YEARS AGO)
In the Cretaceous Period, the dinosaurs were at their peak. Tyrannosaurus Rex and Triceratops lived at this time. Near the end of this period, the dinosaurs became extinct.

In the **Cre**taceous Period, **cre**atures thrive, But by the end of it no dinos are alive!

To remember the order they come in, you could:

Try **j**uggling **cre**am cakes!

That's a Date!

Two-line rhymes can help you to remember important historical dates. You can even put them together for a whole series of events.

This poem will help you remember important events in the 20th century and when they happened:

In **1912**, in April,
The ship **Titanic** was in peril.
From **1914** for over four years,
The **First World War** brought tears.
In the year **1917**,
Russia's Revolution was seen.
From '**39** to '**45**,
World War Two came alive.
In space in **1969**,
Neil Armstrong's **moon landing** was fine.

See if you can come up with some more rhymes for important dates in your life so far.

HISTORICAL WHO'S WHO

Ancient Greek Heroes

Ancient Greece was a world of gods, legends and heroes. This phrase will help you remember six of the most famous ancient Greek heroes:

Jason Or The Odd **Ach**y **Pers**on.
Jason, Orpheus, **The**seus, **Od**ysseus, **Ach**illes, **Pers**eus.

Jason. Jason set sail with a team called the Argonauts, in search of the golden fleece.

Orpheus. This hero famously visited the Underworld to rescue his wife, Eurydice.

Theseus. He killed a beast called the Minotaur, who had been living in a maze and eating children.

Odysseus. He was the hero of Homer's poem, *The Odyssey*, which tells the story of his journey home after the Trojan war.

Achilles. This hero was an invincible warrior who died when an arrow struck his heel – his only weak spot.

Perseus. He killed Medusa, a hideous Gorgon, whose stare turned people to stone.

The Twelve Labours of Hercules

The most famous of all the Greek heroes was Hercules, who completed twelve impossible challenges, known as the Twelve Labours of Hercules. You can remember his tricky tasks with this little poem:

> **Lion**, **Hydra**, **Hind** and **Boar**,
> Clean the **Stables** and off once more.
> **Birds**, **Bull** and **Mares** to battle,
> Catch a **Belt** and then some **Cattle**.
> Golden **Apples** he had to steal,
> Then **Cerberus** to end the deal.

The twelve tasks Hercules had to tackle were: slaying the Nemean Lion and the nine-headed Hydra; capturing a deer that could run really fast, called the Cerynean Hind, and a wild boar; cleaning out some seriously stinky stables; sorting out some man-eating birds; capturing a giant bull; catching some fearsome horses, and stealing the belt of a warrior queen; bringing back a monster's cows, a god's apples; and last but not least, capturing Cerberus, a three-headed dog at the entrance to the Underworld. And you thought your maths homework was tricky!

Explorers and Their Discoveries

You probably already know about Christopher Columbus and his voyage of discovery to America. There's a famous mnemonic rhyme to help you remember when this took place. This begins:

> In fourteen-hundred-and-ninety-two,
> Columbus sailed the ocean blue.
> He had three ships and left from Spain;
> He sailed through sunshine, wind and rain …

But what about other explorers who made important discoveries? This poem will help you remember them.

> So **Columbus** found the new world in **1492**,
> But five years later, **Vasco da Gama** set sail, too.
> He found a new sea route to the **Indian** land,
> Around Africa four ships took his brave band.
> In **1519 Cortes** conquered **Mexico**,
> While off to **Peru Pizarro** did go.
> But the longest voyage is yet to be told,
> **Magellan's round-world trip**, so daring and bold.
> Two hundred and fifty one brave men set sail,
> For three years they voyaged and did not fail,
> In **1522**, they reached home in their ship,
> Only 18 survivors from that long trip.

Inventors and Inventions

History has been changed by some amazing inventions. Where would we be without the wheel, or electric lighting? Make sure you're not in the dark about some of these famous folk:

Alexander Graham Bell (1847 – 1922)

A Scottish inventor, who was fascinated by communication and whose studies led him to invent the first telephone in 1876. To remember who invented the telephone:

👁 *Picture a big **telephone** ringing like a **bell**.*

Thomas Edison (1847 – 1931)

Thomas Edison developed our modern lighting system with a bulb that burned brightly and for a long time. In 1882, he formed the Edison Electric Illuminating Company, and electric lighting began. To remember who invented modern lighting:

👁 *Imagine a man named Eddie congratulating his son Thomas for being so clever.*
('Eddie's-son' sounds like 'Edison'.)

John Logie Baird (1888 – 1946)

In 1924, Baird (pronounced bear – d) invented a machine that could transmit an image over a short distance. This was the birth of the television. To remember who invented TV:

👁 *Imagine a* **bear** *dancing around on your* **television** *screen.*

The Wright Brothers

In 1903, Wilbur and Orville Wright made the first powered air flight for a historic, yet short, 12 seconds. Remember it using this sentence:

The first plane flew (**W**)**right** into the air.

Alexander Fleming (1881 – 1955)

In 1928, Alexander Fleming accidentally discovered the antibiotic penicillin when some mould grew on a petri dish he had left uncovered. Remember:

Fleming didn't make a **pen**ny from his **pen**icillin invention, and yet he saved millions of lives.

BRILLIANT BUILDINGS

Castles

The Medieval Age was a violent, dangerous time to be alive. Kings and powerful lords were constantly waging war as they fought each other for land and wealth.

These kings and lords built huge castles to protect themselves from attack. Although each was different in its design, most were made up of the same parts. These are a **m**oat, a **d**rawbridge, a **p**ortcullis, a **g**atehouse, **b**attlements, an **o**uter **b**ailey, an **i**nner **b**ailey and a **k**eep. Remember:

My Daughter Polly Goes Bonkers On Bananas
In Bubbly Ketchup!

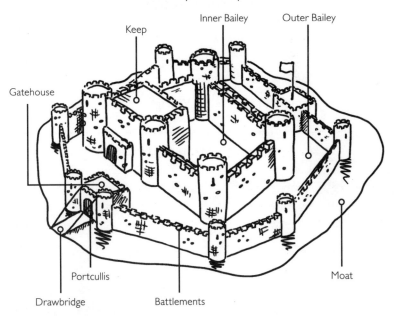

The Tower of London

You can use memory tricks to help you remember the history of any famous landmarks you visit. For example, the Tower of London is now one of London's most famous tourist attractions, but for hundreds of years it was a fortress, where many people were imprisoned. Read on to find out about some of the Tower's most famous prisoners and how to remember them.

THE TWO PRINCES

Young Prince Edward and his little brother Richard were sent to the Tower of London. Edward thought he was waiting to be crowned in a ceremony, but instead his uncle Richard became king and the two little princes were never seen again. Historians believe they were murdered in the Tower.

ANNE BOLEYN

Anne Boleyn was the second wife of King Henry VIII and reigned as Queen of England for three years. She was imprisoned in the Tower, and then beheaded in 1536.

CATHERINE HOWARD

This young woman was Henry VIII's fifth wife and was queen for two years. She was beheaded after her imprisonment.

Elizabeth I

Princess Elizabeth was sent to the Tower when her older sister Mary was on the throne. She was later released and went on to become queen.

Walter Raleigh

Raleigh was a sea-faring explorer and one of the most popular members of Elizabeth I's court. He was imprisoned twice and eventually executed by James I.

Guy Fawkes

Guy Fawkes tried to blow up the Houses of Parliament. His plan failed, and he was sent to the Tower before being executed. The 5th of November in the UK is sometimes called Guy Fawkes' Night, when models of Guy Fawkes are burnt on huge bonfires.

To remember these famous prisoners, use the grouping technique mixed with a rhyme:

> **Two princes**, **two queens** and a young **princess**,
> add **Raleigh** and **Fawkes** and you've got a fine mess!

ART, MUSIC AND LITERATURE

AWESOME ART

Art is all around you, in lots of different forms. Whether you like to get stuck in with drawing, painting or sculpting, or if you prefer to soak up the beautiful masterpieces of artists who've come before you, keep reading to impress your art teacher and make your life more colourful!

The Colour Wheel

A colour wheel will help you to remember how colours work, and how you can mix colours together to make different ones.

The three primary colours – red, blue and yellow – are those that are not made by mixing other colours.

Each of the secondary colours – orange, green and purple – is made by mixing the two primary colours either side of it on the colour wheel. To remember which are primary colours and which are secondary colours, use the rhyme:

First came **red** and **yellow** with their best friend **blue.**

Then came **green** and **orange**, and **purple** came, too.

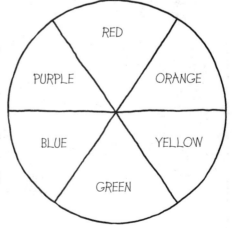

Art Through the Ages

If you study art, you will notice that there have been lots of different artistic styles used by painters and sculptors through the centuries. Use this simple sentence to help you to remember some of them, and then read on to find out a bit more about them:

Painting **A**rt **M**adly **R**eally **B**reaks
Rules = **I**nteresting **P**ictures!

Prehistoric. Prehistoric art dates from around 70,000 BC. Examples of art created by early people include the spectacular paintings in the Lascaux cave in France.

Ancient Art. Examples of ancient art include Roman frescoes and Greek vases.

Middle Ages. Art from the Middle Ages contains many religious scenes and objects.

Renaissance. This style includes works by Leonardo da Vinci, Botticelli and Michelangelo.

Baroque. The Baroque period involved dramatic paintings and sculptures that were sometimes quite sinister.

Romanticism. Art in the Romantic period featured lots of sweeping landscapes.

Impressionism. The Impressionist artists focused on painting scenes as if they'd just caught a glimpse of them. One of the most famous impressionist painters is Claude Monet.

Pop Art. Pop art uses bright colours and geometric shapes. Artists such as Andy Warhol and Roy Lichtenstein showed that anything from soup cans to comic strips could be art.

Six Famous Artworks

Read the poem below, and you'll learn about six of the most famous paintings in the world. If you have a favourite painting or work of art, why not make up a rhyme for it and add it to this poem?

> **Vincent Van Gogh**'s *Sunflowers*,
> Show off the Dutchman's powers.
> While **da Vinci**'s *Mona Lisa*,
> Is certainly sure to please ya!
> **Michelangelo**'s *Sistine* ceiling,
> Shows true artistic feeling,
> And as for **Gustav Klimt**'s *Kiss*,
> That's a painting not to miss.
> *The Scream* by **Edvard Munch**,
> Is the fifth painting in this bunch.
> While **Andy Warhol**'s *Campbell's Soup*,
> Finishes this famous group.

MARVELLOUS MUSIC

Get ready to brush up your knowledge and impress people with your amazing musical memory.

Parts of an Orchestra

An orchestra usually contains four types of instrument. These are: **s**tring instruments, such as the violin; **p**ercussion, which are instruments that you can hit or shake; **w**oodwind instruments, such as the clarinet, and **b**rass instruments, such as the trumpet and the trombone.

Remember these types of instruments by using the phrase:

Symphonies **P**layed **W**ith **B**rilliance.

Music, Maestro!

These memory tricks will help you to remember more about the instruments that make beautiful music in an orchestra.

STRINGS AND THINGS

To remember the most important string instruments in an orchestra, use the sentence:

Viola's **violin** said, '**Cello**' to the **double bass**.

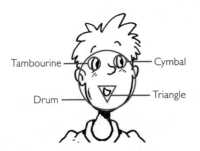

Tambourine — Cymbal

Drum — Triangle

BEAT IT!

To help you remember percussion instruments:

👁 *Picture a face, made from a drum, with a cymbal and a tambourine for eyes and a triangle for a mouth!*

BLOW YOUR OWN TRUMPET

The following mnemonic will help you to remember four of the most important brass instruments:

The drinking **horn** held three teas ('**t**'s)

The three '**t**'s are the **t**uba, the **t**rumpet and the **t**rombone.

TOOT THE FLUTE

Woodwind instruments may look very similar, but you can remember the names of some of them with this little rhyme:

Clarinet, **oboe** and **bassoon**,
Piccolo, **flute** and **saxophone**.

GET IT WRITE!

Get ready to beat even the biggest bookworm, as you learn how to remember some of the most famous works of literature.

Potty for Potter

Harry Potter and his wizarding adventures have entertained millions of readers. Use the following little story to help you remember all seven books in the right order.

Harry Potter was out walking when he tripped over a **stone** (*The Philosopher's **Stone***). He noticed a hidden trapdoor that led him to a **chamber** (*The **Chamber** Of Secrets*), where there was a **prisoner** (*The **Prisoner** Of Azkaban*) chained up inside. In the corner of the room was a roaring **fire** (*The Goblet Of **Fire***). Suddenly a **phoenix** (*The Order Of The **Phoenix***) flew from the flames and transformed into a handsome **prince** (*The Half Blood **Prince***). Harry was so shocked that all he could say was, '**Hallo!**' (*The Deathly **Hallo**ws.*)

Shakespeare's Plays

William Shakespeare wrote some of the most famous plays of all time. This poem will help you to remember them.

Let's learn them **As You Like It**,
Without a **Comedy Of Errors**,
From the **Merry Wives Of Windsor**
To **Macbeth** and other terrors.
There's **Othello** and **King John**,
And there's **Hamlet** and **King Lear**,
Young **Romeo And Juliet**,
Who loved with a love so dear.
Henry IV Parts One and Two,
Henry V is another,
Henry VI One, Two and Three
And **Henry VIII** the other.
Richard II and **Richard III**,
Are other kings from the bard's pen,
There's **Two Gentlemen Of Verona**,
And even **Two Noble Kinsmen**.
He wrote of **Julius Caesar**,
Cymbeline and **Pericles**, too,
He told of **Titus Andronicus**,
And of the **Taming Of The Shrew**.
From a cool **Midsummer Night's Dream**,
To **The Tempest** and **A Winter's Tale**,
From **Timon Of Athens** in Greece,
To **The Merchant Of Venice** we sail.
There's the tale of **Love's Labour's Lost**,
And that of **Measure For Measure**,
There's **Much Ado About Nothing**,
And **Twelfth Night** is a real treasure.
Of **Troilus And Cressida**,
And **Coriolanus** I tell,
Of **Antony And Cleopatra**,
But **All's Well That Ends Well**.

OTHER STUFF

A LITTLE BIT OF EVERYTHING

The other sections in this book will help your marvellous memory to be the best in the classroom. This one will boost your general knowledge for when school's out, so you'll always be ready to impress your friends with your terrific trivia.

One for Sorrow

There are many superstitions that give meanings to everyday things. For example, you probably know that the number 13 is supposed to be unlucky. Some superstitions are more detailed, and need mnemonics to help people remember the meanings attached to them. Read the poem below to decode the meanings behind groups of magpies.

> One for sorrow, two for joy,
> Three for a girl, four for a boy,
> Five for silver, six for gold,
> Seven for a secret never to be told,
> Eight for a wish, nine for a kiss,
> Ten for a bird that's best to miss.

The Decathlon

The toughest athletic competition of all is the decathlon. Athletes have to compete in not just one, but ten track and field events! Here's a handy way to learn the sports that make up the contest, using the grouping technique.

Most athletics events involve running, jumping or throwing, so group the events in this order:

Three runs (100 metres, 400 metres, 1,500 metres).
Three jumps (long jump, high jump, pole vault).
Three throws (discus, javelin, shotput).

You might have noticed that this only adds up to nine events but, as long as you remember these, you'll have no problem getting over the last **hurdle** (the tenth event is the 110 metre hurdles).

The Parts of a Ship

Sailors use different words to describe the front, back, left and right of a ship. Use the following mnemonic – starting at the front of the ship and moving clockwise:

Bow to the **star**s (starboard),
turn (stern) to **port**.

Did You Know?
It is said that the word 'posh' is an acronym for '**P**ort **O**ut, **S**tarboard **H**ome,' and was used by wealthy passengers on long sea journeys to help them remember where to book the best cabins.

Types of Coffee

Coffee can be served with milk, with foam, even with chocolate! The different combinations of coffee and milk have different names. Read on to wow your friends with your sophisticated knowledge of coffee culture!

Espresso. This is a shot of pure black coffee, served in a tiny cup without milk.

Macchiato. This strong coffee drink is served in a small cup, with a shot of espresso and a small amount of steamed milk.

Americano. An Americano is a shot of espresso, served in a large mug and topped up with hot water.

Latte. If you order a latte, you'll be served a large cup filled with espresso and steamed milk, then topped with foamy milk.

Cappucino. This coffee is a shot of espresso, topped with lots of foaming milk and sometimes chocolate shavings.

Mocha. A decadent mocha contains espresso, chocolate, steamed milk and sometimes a blob of whipped cream.

Remember the different coffees with the sentence:

Even Meerkats Are Late
Counting Money!

Signs of the Zodiac

Astrologists are people who believe people are influenced by the position of groups of stars at the time of their birth. The 12 constellations they use are called the Zodiac. Check out your star sign below and find out how to remember all 12.

Aries   The Ram   21 March – 20 April
Taurus   The Bull   21 April – 20 May
Gemini   The Twins   21 May – 20 June
Cancer   The Crab   21 June – 20 July
Leo   The Lion   21 July – 22 August
Virgo   The Virgin   23 August – 22 September
Libra   The Scales   23 September – 22 October
Scorpio   The Scorpion   23 October – 22 November
Sagittarius The Archer   23 November – 23 December
Capricorn   The Goat   23 December – 20 January
Aquarius   The Water Carrier 21 January – 19 February
Pisces   The Fish   20 February – 20 March

You can use the first letter of each of the Zodiac signs to make a mega acrostic sentence, like this one:

All **T**he **G**reen **C**ats **L**ike **V**ery **L**arge **S**caly **S**almon **C**anned **A**nd **P**ickled.

Or, to remember the order with a picture

👁 *Imagine a clock face. Picture Aries (a ram) at number 12, and go around clockwise, replacing each number with a Zodiac sign.*

Ranks of the Army

The armed forces need to be very well organized indeed if they are to be effective. This is why having different ranks is so important. There are many ranks in the army, but there are nine main divisions. These, in order of importance, are: General, Brigadier, Colonel, Major, Captain, Lieutenant, Sergeant, Corporal and Private.

The following poem will help you to remember them in the right order.

'In **general**,' the **Brigadier** to the **Colonel** said,
'The **major** problem's the **Captain**, who stays in bed.
The **Lieutenant** is lazy, so the **Sergeant** taught us,
And the **Corporal**'s asleep in his **private** quarters.'

Phases of the Moon

As the moon travels round the Earth, it seems to change. Night by night, the part of the moon you see grows (waxes) from a thin crescent-shape to a full circle and then shrinks (wanes) back once more to a thin crescent before disappearing. The cycle then begins again. These changes are called the phases of the moon. To recognize the phases when the moon is in the night sky, use the word **DOC**.

Shape Of The Moon	Shaped Like A Letter	Phase
	D	Waxing
	O	Full
	C	Waning

THE
MEMORY GYM

TERRIFIC TECHNIQUES

This book contains a whole range of mnemonic devices to help you remember information – poems, pictures, acrostics, numbers, patterns, phrases, sayings, puns, wordplay, stories and journeys. Hopefully, you will be able to start using some of these tricks for other memory tasks you come across.

In this section of the book, you'll find some other techniques you can use and some games you can play to give your memory skills a good workout.

Chunking

Chunking is used to group items together to give you fewer 'bits' to remember. For example, if you had to remember the number 703861952, it is a much easier task if you try to remember it as:

703 – 861 – 952.

The reason it is easier is because you are tricking your brain into thinking it only has to remember three things instead of nine.

You can combine chunking with chants or rhymes to make it even more effective. Take, for example, the seven dwarfs from Disney's *Snow White*: **S**neezy, **S**leepy, **D**opey, **D**oc, **H**appy, **B**ashful and **G**rumpy.

You can use chunking to remember them by using the chant:

Double **S**, Double **D** and an **HBG**!

Number Rhyming

Number rhyming is really useful when you need to remember a list of items, such as when you go shopping.

To use number rhyming, you start by thinking of ten things that rhyme with the numbers from one to ten. Examples are given below, but making up your own rhymes is even better:

One rhymes with **Sun**
Two rhymes with **glue**
Three rhymes with **tree**
Four rhymes with **door**
Five rhymes with **hive**
Six rhymes with **sticks**
Seven rhymes with **heaven**
Eight rhymes with **gate**
Nine rhymes with **sign**
Ten rhymes with **pen.**

Imagine your mother has sent you into your local supermarket and asked you to buy the following items: bananas, cake, lemonade, jelly, chocolate, spaghetti, beefburgers, bacon and bread. She has told you that you can buy yourself a comic as well, while you are there.

Link up each of the items on your shopping list with a number from one to ten, and remember your number rhyme that goes with it. Then, picture the scene in your mind, and it's sure to stay there.

This may seem like even more things to remember, but you'll find it's a system that really works!

For example, bananas are first on your list, so they're number one. Remember that **one** rhymes with **Sun**.

👁 *Imagine the **Sun**, with its rays made up of **bananas**!*

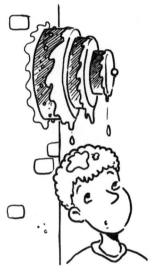

Cake is next on the shopping list, so that's number two. Remember that **two** rhymes with **glue**.

👁 *Picture a birthday **cake glued** to the wall!*

Carry on creating pictures in your head until you've completed the shopping list.

Once you have pictured all the scenes, see if you can remember all the objects. You should find you remember far more of the items on your list this way.

The Memory Palace

The memory palace helps you to remember items by wandering through a wonderful building that you have created in your imagination.

To practise the memory palace, read on to learn about the Seven Wonders of the Ancient World. These are: the Great Pyramid of Giza, the Hanging Gardens of Babylon, the Colossus of Rhodes, the Mausoleum of Halicarnassus, the Pharos of Alexandria, the Statue of Zeus and the Temple of Artemis.

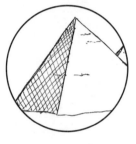

👁 *Imagine walking through the front door of your palace. You're standing in a huge hallway, where a* **great Egyptian** *Pharaoh greets you. (The Great Pyramid)*

From the hall you walk up a wide staircase. At the top, a **baby** *in a pram holds out a* **flower** *to you. (The Hanging Gardens of* **Baby***lon)*

You reach the top of the staircase and see two corridors disappearing off like long **roads***. (The Colossus of Rhodes)*

*You walk along a corridor to a big window looking out on to the grounds where there is a large pond. You look out and see a **hali**but turning **car**twheels. (The Mausoleum of **Halicar**nassus)*

*You turn a corner and enter a grand banquetting hall. A waitress named **Alexandria** offers you a tiny model of a **lighthouse** on a silver platter. (The Pharos of Alexandria)*

*Leaving the hall, you walk down three steps and into a busy kitchen, full of people running to and fro preparing a delicious meal fit for the god **Zeus**. (The Statue of Zeus)*

*The chef chases you away, and you run into a room, where the mistress of the palace is painting a work of art at an easel. She's an **arty miss**! (The Temple of Artemis)*

You have now completed your walk through the palace. Now, imagine going back to the front door and repeating your journey. See if you can see all the objects that help you remember each of the Seven Wonders of the World.

Once you get the hang of a memory palace, you can use it to remember absolutely anything.

THE GAMES ROOM

Playing games can be a great way to give your memory a really good workout. The games below will help you to develop your memory muscles and have some fun, too.

___

Memory

To play 'Memory', all you need is a pack of cards, a good memory and an opponent.

Shuffle the cards and lay all of them face down in four rows of 13. The object of the game is to find more matching pairs than your opponent. A matching pair is two cards of the same value and the same colour. For example, the seven of clubs and the seven of spades would be a matching pair, as would the queen of diamonds and the queen of hearts.

How to play: Player One picks a card and turns it over so both players can see it. He then turns over a second card. If they form a matching pair, he wins the cards, puts them in his pile and has another turn. If they are not a matching pair, they are returned, face down, to their place in the rows.

Player Two now turns over a card. If the card matches one of those turned over by Player One, she can turn that card over to make a pair. Otherwise, she turns over a different card.

As the game continues, it is important to remember the location and value of as many of the cards that have been turned over as possible. This will help you find more pairs than your opponent. Play continues until all the cards have been matched. The winner is the person with the most pairs.

I Went to Market and Bought ...

How to play: The first player thinks of an item to start the list. For example she might say: 'I went to market and bought a bucket.'

The next player adds an item: 'I went to market and bought a bucket and a tin of sardines.'

Play continues with each person adding an item:

'I went to market and bought a bucket, a tin of sardines, a guitar ...'

If someone forgets an item, they are out of the game. Play continues until there is only one person left.

I'm Sure There's Something Missing!

This game will help you develop your visual memory. Collect a dozen or so objects and lay them out on a tray. You can use anything you like – pens, paper clips, sweets, rulers, bits of paper, cups and so on.

How to play: Show the tray to the other player and allow them 20 seconds to study it. Then ask them to turn around so they cannot see what you're doing.

Pick an object and remove it from the tray, then shuffle the objects and then ask the person to turn around and tell you which item is missing.

The other player then chooses a group of items and it is your turn to try to remember which item is missing.

What's Happening?

'What's Happening?' is another game that helps develop your visual memory.

How to play: Find a picture that shows a lot of activity, such as the street scene opposite. Allow the other player to study it for a minute. Next, hold the picture so that your friend cannot see it and ask ten questions to see how well he has remembered it. For example, in the scene on the next page, your questions could include:

1. How many people are wearing hats?
2. What is the name of the butcher's shop?
3. What is the dog doing?
4. Who is riding a bike?
5. What is the time?
6. What is the number of the bus?
7. What type of holiday is on the travel agent's poster?
8. What are the two men carrying?
9. Who is wearing a scarf?
10. How many birds are there?